BLACK AND WHITE

Also by William Scammell

POETRY

Yes and No (1979)
A Second Life (1982)
Jouissance (1985)
Eldorado (1987)
Bleeding Heart Yard (1992)
The Game: Tennis Poems (1992)
Five Easy Pieces (1993)
Barnacle Bill (1994)
All Set to Fall Off the Edge of the World (1998)

CRITICISM

Keith Douglas: A Study (1988)

AS EDITOR

Between Comets: For Norman Nicholson at 70 (1984)
The New Lake Poets (1991)
Poetry Book Society Anthology 3 (1992)
This Green Earth (1992)
Ted Hughes: Winter Pollen (1993)

BLACK AND WHITE

William Scammell

Acknowledgements

Some of these poems have appeared in the following publications:
New Writing 10 (ed. Penelope Lively and George Szirtes,
Picador in association with the British Council, 2001),
Other Poetry, *Pitch*, *Poetry Ireland*, *Quadrant* (Australia)
and *Thumbscrew*.

First published in England in 2002 by Flambard Press
Stable Cottage, East Fourstones, Hexham NE47 5DX

Typeset by Harry Novak
Front cover image: 'Hawthorn', charcoal drawing by Alan Stones
Cover design by Gainford Design Associates
Printed in England by Cromwell Press, Trowbridge, Wiltshire

A CIP catalogue record for this book
is available from the British Library.

ISBN 1 873226 54 3

Flambard Press wishes to thank Northern Arts
for its financial support.

Website: www.flambardpress.co.uk

WILLIAM NEIL SCAMMELL

1939–2000

Introduction

Black and White consists of two sections, the first of which contains the poems Bill had already listed for a new collection.

It is clear that Bill wanted other poems to be included, and those in Section II are from the file he was working on in his final year. His wife Jan, his elder son Ben, and I, with the approval of his other son Chris, have chosen to print many of those in this file, as well as a few extra ones from a handmade illustrated collection of typed poems called 'Jan's Book', which Bill listed on a scrap of paper headed USE. In certain cases, the typescripts and manuscripts contained alternative words or phrases, and where it wasn't immediately apparent which Bill had decided on, we have opted for those we think he would have chosen.

Christopher Pilling

Contents

I

II

I

Black and White

Here's my mother in her 1920s
cloche hat and coat, trimmed
with fake fur and ending
precisely at the knee.
She's balanced in semi-high heels
with one strap across the instep,
her left leg taking the weight,
the other one held out, slightly
pointed, as though to be young
was to be in a ballet, and
the hands clasped in front of her
might be summoned any minute
by massed violins, and turn to wings.

Is it okay to love your mother
when she's eighteen and you're sixty,
presumed innocent? Was it okay
for her to confide her infinity
of problems in me, as though she
was still in the air, and I might catch her?

Heft

The heft, the haft, the shaft
of the axe, the ankle, calf
muscle and polished thigh
of the axe, its cut and thrust,
its invitation to the waltz,
the grin of the edge, the recidivist
lump at the back of the head,
the creak of oak, spit of sap,
split skirt of bark,
the high cheekbones, Luluesque
pallor, hard-knock hips,
the sheer stocking tops,
the hammer horror of the axe
caught in a fix, a cleft stick –
the bondage of labour, and
the sweetly humped back.

Mowdy

The dead march as wedding march,
the veil rent by perfect gloom,
a small Valley of the Kings
tenebrous and warm.

Matter toiling along
at no miles per hour,
a river of black light unlit
by anything we can bring to bear.

All we shall get
of the cross of the mole
is the dark skylight, the tilt
underfoot, the tell-tale

operations of blind fate as it
steps under the lawn
heading for your instep
one scratch at a time.

Litany

Peace to their flat tweed caps,
their battered pickups, their 1930s
trousers and turn-ups, their waiting dogs,
humble as a patchwork rug.
Peace to the golem of their noses
pitted against all the devils above and below,
the ambivalent nods, the odds and sods
of jobs that are born needing doing again.
Peace to the ammoniac stench of piss
that moats the barn in winter,
the infinite spaces of the rain-barrel,
cobblestones hunched down for the long haul.
Peace to the long hours in his head,
the naked light bulb in the yard.

The Mountain

There's more of it than you think, and more
even than that, once you set foot
on the upward path, driven by what is
and what isn't, an eye that startles
upwards, winging the ghylls and gullies,
the buttresses, ribs and rocky spines,
those dreary stretches in between
one outcrop and the next, the succession
of ridges and tops that aren't tops at all,
the becks flashing scuts as they leap
and fall, the mountain ash's homely touch,
straight from the rock, conjuring
leaves out of hard-hearted geology,
waving you on past the diamond white
of the pool to some notional triumph
at the top where uplift is assured, for birds
at any rate, for the cairn of stones
and triangulation point, for the first man –
Petrarch was it? – who walked up a mountain
for fun, or so they say, where the world
lay at his feet, renounced or embraced,
his arms swinging, the big calf muscles
lifting him up from the Strand or Via Dolorosa,
clear out of his kind, so that he might
put his head in the clouds and take in the view.

Higham Hall

Down past the Himalayan cedar
staring out over Bass Lake to Skiddaw
and round behind fulsome rhododendrons
there's a laburnum tree in full spate,
humming with bees like a synagogue.
It's so pretty I jump back in disbelief
and then approach as though it was a burning bush.
The warden's put its Latin name on a plaque
so you can take your pick between
mind and matter, though the tree's long since
torn up these things with its hands and thrown
them away. Best go with the look-at-me
blossoms, this impossible lantern
sailing over an English lawn
towards the Strawberry Hill Gothic house
(blood on its scutcheon, flowers in its purse)
ardent for summer, happy to ship
you off to native or to foreign parts
just by standing still, breaking out
the one language you never knew you spoke.

Blue Movie

Tim lets loose a couple of rams
in his yard brimming with sheep
skittering about on tiptoe like surfers
who have spotted the seventh wave.
Now I know where the phrase
battering-ram comes from.
There's nothing dainty about it, nothing
to say whether this crossing of one breed
with another will result in the 'comely maidens'
of Eamon de Valera's dream state
or the advanced daughters of America,
steering only by higher education
and a garniture of ethnic earrings.

The cockerel goes by on stilts, fresh
from the colourist, who's teased out his plumes.
Throaty suggestions float down from pigeons.
Moles have exclaimed all over the lawn.
The farmyard rocks to its blue movie

while back at our place there's man-woman
stuff to be dealt with, which drives you
to précis the Bible in your own hand
and me to flutter over the cafetière.
Injury hangs mute, left over from
yesterday. A great baa-ing fills
the room, or would do if we opened up,
the strictly human baa of right and wrong,
thin as India paper, the wrong tack entirely
for our next jump over the moon.
It's time we both came clean. Out there
is the clothes line tethering us
to mother nature, looped from the drainpipe
to a tangle of wild plums. Your bright
cotton knickers are taking the air
like small sails bound for Ithaca.

Ted's Funeral

A full round orange moon
is up on its elbows
looking through trees

like a baby just woken up
not sure where it is
drinking in space.

This was later,
three hundred and fifty miles on
from you in Devon

clapped in an oak box;
a long, long way north
from me and Olwyn

having a fag in the garden
of Court Green, where
the head man of Faber

and *The Times* editor were nodding
together, and Carol
slipped out of a side door

in her wellies, making for
the veg (her hand in mine
a coin of ice),

and Mr and Mrs Seamus
came slowly out on the wet cobbles
for a breath of air.

It was all accidental,
harmonious, coincidental,
like my son Ben

landing on the edge of the aura
of Paul Muldoon
in the upstairs room

heaving with names;
like this big
unexpected moon

on the night of your funeral,
daring you not to lay down
the cloak of your life

while she climbs up
through a crown of leaves.
Outside there were policemen

in capes, as though dodged
out of a John Buchan novel,
a few half-hearted paparazzi

not knowing who was who.
What with an organ
dribbling half-hearted notes

into the boxy, foursquare
Protestant silence,
the rain immediately after

scattering mourners
like minnows
before they could reform

and glide together
on a wave of grief,
the long dark haul uphill

to Cumbria in the outside lane,
dazed by speed
and immobility,

this gross physical ache,
the nameless faculty
of disbelief, as if

someone had put a No Entry
sign up on your name,
or wiped out an entire song,

I was in need of
illumination, and the moon
obliged, tilting my head up

to catch sight
of a second sight
there at my finger ends

paired with the dark.

Tauromachia

Half a ton of idleness, the bull
is lying down by the fence
with his harem sunk round him
at a respectful distance.

Which way the magnetism goes
isn't altogether clear,
whether they've got him by the nose
or he's felled them with a stare.

It's that time of year, anyway,
when the bull and the ram
put in their stiff-legged
appearance on the farm

all muscle and sperm and defiance,
barrelling out of prison,
looking straight through animal science,
English heritage, feminism

to the mud-caked houris
of the opposite sex
awaiting them in paradise
with long languorous backs.

Personally I wouldn't wish
a china shop on any bull,
nor Aesop, nor a suit of lights.
My bull is categorical,

which is to say he has corners
you can't see round, a head quarried
out of some old language
long since buried

under four-wheelers and bar-codes,
those capitalist fugues.
Any road, the demon gets up
slowly, takes to his legs

and stalks off in the lawful
manner of a bull,
the life model gone walkabout,
standing to on the brow of a hill.

His ghost's down there, clamped
deep in the fissured rock,
all ochres and outlines, dancing since
dreamtime, dancing the Lord knows what.

The Raincoat

Kippered in cigarette smoke
and needled with marginalia
my first editions won't be worth much
to my heirs, nor the letters and biographies,
the tasteful pictures, the one-off brass
musician and stone goddess
of doubtful provenance and mythic
fecundity, bought somewhere east
of Tunis on a windy Thursday
when the Med churned up heaps
of seaweed on a ploughed, empty beach
three-quarters clean again next day.

That was then. Now the big logs outside
stick together, cauterised by frost,
as though one sawing was enough.
It seems cruel to tread on the icy grass.
Blade-cold and sunny under a high
blue dome, the vaunted crystal firmament.
This is how it was in the old days,
before we cooked up the meridians into rain.

Here's a blackbird scuttling in
on his broomstick, quick as a flash,
quicker than his own startled call.

And here's you in the old raincoat
down to your ankles, that witching hair,
come to see what marriage looks like
in the open air.

David's Grand

If you have one at home the living room
has to be organised round it, as a politician's
year bends around parliament, or the sink
commands a kitchen.

Showing off its curves one minute, or its teeth,
then settling down to the serious business
of sawing life in half

as though one hand following the sun
wasn't enough without the other hand
chipping in its two-penn'orth of darkness,
the under-mind

balancing those sweet trills, high-lofted Bach
setting a thousand prayer-wheels going
in dome and crypt.

This is high opera for every man,
an ivory tower, a portable Bayreuth
crashing out great harmonies, great
slabs of light

hammering like furies on a lacquered black
body with the butterfly kiss
whispering secrets, anxious to get things
off its chest.

What it proposes is marriage and a mortgage.
You can't very well divorce
promise, its vast spiritual upkeep
or your purse.

God frayed us into fingers, it seems,
and the hand responds as best it can.
Witness David, straight-backed among the arpeggios,
running flat out

after both parts of that tune.

The Taste of Epic

We were coming to the end of Book One
of *The Faerie Queene*
when a full eclipse of the moon
began, so we trooped out onto the lawn
to watch. This was not long
after meeting Death, the suicide canto
where old Mister Death, *with thornes*
together pind and patched, is found
selling *sleepe after toyle, port after*
stormie seas, ease after warre.

The one who'd said
allegory is dead had gone off
in his Nissan. The rest of us
stretched our necks, trying out
feelings appropriate to an eclipse.

The moon kept its side
of the bargain, pulling over itself
a hood of darkness, very slowly,
while we scurried about with a tele-
scope, binoculars, the naked eye,
heads tilted back like radars
fogged with the quanta of streetlights,
calendars, predictions, digital
watches, insulated against ourselves
by four hundred years of exact science.

Not Forgetting the Dog

Late August, and the evening isn't sure
whether it burns in summer or in autumn fire.
Low sun flames through the trees; a single thought
unites four players on the tennis court.
Beside them in the long grass, through the mesh,
a collie crouches patiently, his face
all triangles, his limitless tolerance
extending from the midges to the human dance
they dance so badly that he almost sighs.
In marble though, in blinks and courtesies
somewhere between a Pharaoh and a slave
tending the darkness, so the sun might live.

Worms

i.m. Geoffrey Holloway

Archie Ammons has this poem called 'geezerly'
about being too old to squat any more
so that he can rescue an earthworm
from a puddle and put it back on the floor

of the earth. I'm not that old yet but
I begin to know what he means.
I can't scratch the middle of my back.
My legs don't prosper any more in jeans.

I can run, but not like the little girl I saw
skittering along in the middle of town,
soaring over the cracks in the pavement
two, three, four at a time

with her head half-turned knowingly
on its stalk to crack a wicked smile at me,
like Anna Pavlova swanning along
on a muscle, a moonbeam, and a song.

There wasn't an illness in the body's chest
of illnesses that Geof didn't know about,
from tiny intimations of the last gasp
to the poor man's itch and rich man's gout

and that other one only a bike or a bus
ride away, a sense of the ridiculous,
when flesh takes hold of our best thoughts
and asks what's in them, more than dust?

He was especially up on love and its
wrigglings in the two arms of right and wrong
when age breaks down into its lurid bits
and pieces, our fellow feeling for a worm.

Goa

Since there is no elephant
or Mercedes to be had
the family is abroad
on a Vespa, all five of them
rippling through the early dark,
mother and baby gliding along
side-saddle on the back.

*

The banyan tree drops down aerial
roots, enlarges itself in creepers,
making a temple of its own limbs,
a hanging garden, a torrent of suggestions;
plumps up space the way a dancer does,
the way a sitar plucks notes out of its belly
and hugs them, not sure where sorrow ends
and the rest of the world begins.

*

A trumpet sounds at the hotel gates
and there stands Ganesh himself
taller than you'd ever imagined,
parked up on his legs, fronting
the cameras, eyes lost and whalish
in that great head, dumb as the flames
they broke him with, which blacken
the pillars of my chest.

*

In the paddy fields they put and take
all day, bent over the eye of a needle
that stitches them to earth, warm hungry mud,
the long field path, straight as a rod.

*

Inflorescence of a Matisse
languorous on cerulean blue:
the bay as a hedonist masterpiece.

The palms have nothing to say to this.
Why should they? Beauty is all ours.
They lean upwards, as the law insists,
watching the ocean mop its muddy floors.

*

The lads go on hammering long poles
into sand, weaving their shady roofs
out of such handy materials
as the spiky, biodegradable leaves

of the spirit, recommended by gurus
everywhere, lest we think we are gods,
renting the sahib his sunbed and pillows
or selling him soapstone bits and bobs.

These are the one-off cafés, built each year
in a couple of days by quick and practised hands
to service the restless boulevardier
walking his cut-out shadow across the sand.

They riffle off notes with the head of Gandhi
bent over the spindle of his wheel,
all wire-rim specs, and self-sufficiency,
the ghost of that non-violent smile.

*

The fingers are drumming, drumming
under those exquisite ragas,
the heel of the hand for thunder
rained down by unforgiving gods.

Gold for the gypsy women, gold and silk
riotous against oily black
hair and skin, done up as slaves
to mock the slavery of wives.

Self Improvement

'our twentieth century that was going to improve on all the others' – Wislawa Szymborska

for John Lucas

Fifteen. Foxed with acne and loneliness
but entranced down in the gloom of second-hand
bookshops, where things started at threepence.
The rooms went on and on like the inside of a pyramid.

Nobody seemed to want to actually sell. They crabbed
around behind thick lenses and old tweed suits
or cabbage-coloured smocks, looking at you
and the catch hauled to the counter as if not sure

which was the more dubious. You could buy yards
of Victorian fiction, *Curiosities of English Literature*
in microscopic double entry. Meredith's heady periods
were cold porridge now but Thomas Love Peacock

lived up to the promise of his name. What is it
about sentences, whole thrones and dominions of them,
a voice that leads you on like a path into woods
saying I know more about your life than you do?

That'll be ten bob – one third of my week's pay – said
the sepulchral buckram face, and I'd stagger
out with half my bodyweight in letterpress.
Nowadays I'm like a government department, immovable,

weighed down with precedents and dust, a heap
of minds over the coals of a veiny hand. Only
the other day Gibbon reminded me that the founder
of the Inquisition was named Innocent III.

To get to me now you'd have to take your pick
and spade over the sand and look for an entrance.
Here are the vessels for my journey, CDs mostly,
a telephone and fax machine, invites to book parties

I never get to. The mummy cloths are made out
of paper clips. I lie here like one of T.S. Eliot's cheeses,
sweating slightly. Some fine new mind will be along
to eat me soon, smelling of paper and glue, with

verbs for teeth, a stomach set on magnetic north,
a rucksack full of useful conjunctions. Come along
quick, it says, and we'll see if we can find you. Where
did you last see yourself? And where were you hoping to go?

Look at Me

Chardin: *Self-Portrait*, 1775

A Mr Rubicund if ever I saw one,
something between a beekeeper and
one of those gentlemen of substance
who mean to keep science out of the laboratory
and in the studio, where it belongs.
I am transfixed by your cravat,
like a genie out of its bottle
greeting democracy with a flourish,
the Enlightenment spectacles, looking
as though they might very well
have summoned the animals to be named,
and the imperturbable nose in the middle
of it all. Yes I like your nose
best of all, red with sun or wine,
great-great-grandson of Rembrandt's,
cooked up like magma, and then cooled,
pointing you in the direction of your fellow creatures
but intransitive too, like a hill or a fruit,
father of all the noses you carried with you
from the white bulb in the wicker cradle
to the spreading chestnut of your maturity.
I should say the only word for it is *smudged*,
much like the cheeks of the little girl
learning to read in 'The Young Schoolmistress'.
The question then arises, why am I moved
by a smudge? And Chardin gives me
one of those looks, as much as to say
what do you think you think with, if not flesh?

Inside Story

'one of those perfect writers who never write' – Derek Mahon

Once you pick up a pen
there's no end to what might have been,
the novels that came to you in a flash
departing very slowly in peace,

the exemplary studies of great souls
fretting their way out through the bellies of whales,
rearrangements of space and time
to suit the wearer. Certainly I'm

not about to spill more ink
on the gilded ones in the goldfish tank,
deprived of weather as they are,
taking a glass bowl for Antarctica.

Where do they go to, all those infant
meanings eager for epic? Moment by moment
the year breaks and is gone;
the only pattern is the lack of one.

Eerie ambivalence of the light that shines,
or falters in a writer's sweated lines,
the literal fallen into the dark
and slumbering big time, belly up.

Time

Time has been very coy
about Andrew Marvell, what
he did or didn't get up to

in the Baroque, when swords
were theology, kissing hands
off, and my liege lords

galloped about in hot blood
to debate the realm
with their employer. God

had the best view of all
these forensics. Old versus new
and furious charities,

never to be settled, only post-
poned into the bloodstream
of the Augustans and lost

in transit between them and us.
It's all a mist now, remote
as Hector and Patroclus

yet once as real as Belfast,
Divis, Bloody Sunday
and the crouching priest

appealing for calm,
leading the crocodile on
to the safety of home.

So what did the milk-white poet,
MP for Hull, Milton's pal,
the assiduous and persistent

comrade of song make of this
crookback and bloody war
breaking the king's peace?

Cut to members Foot and Benn
flourishing their periods
against late capitalism,

the eco-warriors' God
of dissent still on the *qui vive*
in good Berkshire mud,

the people's duress,
the people's natural skinheads
and the people's princess.

Watch the mucky truth
lifted on dainty silverware
to the poet's mouth.

Am I one of them?
Or one of us?

A Touch of the Goldbergs

Andras Schiff playing 'The Goldberg Variations'

Here's Andras letting the grass grow under Bach,
taking the shine off the carriage work,

seeing the wig blow away into cumulo-nimbus,
bowed over the naked tips of fingers

gliding along in the orbit of that tune
which flies apart, like the phases of the moon.

Here's Andras, I say, an old Rolls Royce
purring along in the best of taste

and I don't think Schubert was invented then
to skim the cream off his deep dark pain

but he's here in spirit. All music's here –
classic   romantic   pious   pedantic –

in the grand old *meister*. Wouldn't you say?
Come, let's put Mahler out of his misery,

that great white elephant of Teutonic noise.
And Bruckner the Humble, down on his hands and knees.

Who's got the time? Majestic, true,
but going on and on forever and a day

as though, once Wagner sobbed, the height of things
was measured by time and a thousand violins.

Come! Let's grow up enough to listen in
to reason. Andras, play that thing again!

Directions for the Preparation and Consumption of Fresh Sweet Corn

Plunge in boiling water for thirty seconds,
lightly salted, free of lobsters,
bubbling only more bubbles,
and serve on a clean white plate
with an extravagant rim.

Now you can pick it up
and play the same chords
over and over on your front teeth.
It starts fast, quite fast
then tails off into thoughtfulness.

Kafka wrote once of the Wish to Be
a Red Indian. Could this be it?
If I look at a moustache long enough
will it begin to explain itself?

II

1939

All the men were born in waistcoats
that buttoned up down the front.
They parted their hair to one side or the other,
not too much of it, licked down with grease.
You could get hold of them by their ears
and their accents. A ten-bob note made
a temporary lord, with title to the full bottle
or a riotous day in Brighton.
Women's fingers pounded typewriters, unwrinkled
stockings, cracked open eggs that were sure
to fluff up into rosy-fingered cakes.
Still in use: flat cloth caps, planing
off the top of the head,
the bolt-on cellular collar, squeezing
the neck like a bastinado,
the moustache, the Austin Seven, fathers
pecking out their sons' livers while appearing
to take an interest only in their futures,
foxtrots executed on sprung dance floors,
the wireless, the locked ward,
the last waltz, the leather strap, the bobby's
bicycle and whistle, potato-picking,
cobblers, tinkers, lace-up leather footballs
with pink bladders for a heart.

Everything was fixed, like a bayonet,
or a Marcel wave, a lipsticked smile.
All you had to do was square back –
another brick in the wall.

The Fire

The fire leapt, the garden turned right round and bit me.
My first real long trousers, my teenage *démarche*...
I fought my own war with my wishes, and lost it.
I screamed, and ran screaming, a bright human torch

and my mother, good angel, came rushing like storm-wind
and threw me down under her, apron and all,
and bore me again, as the flames licked her belly.
My brains fell to rubble. I was a brick wall

for a day or two; then I came back to the surgeons
who'd patched up the pilots. They scraped off my thighs
and wound them around the last sliver of tendon
that lived on the bone; and I opened my eyes.

More angels, weak fruit juice. I was a barked poplar
in need of much watering, swaddled in white.
I put forth new shoots, in the form of hard plaster.
Whenever I wriggled, the plaster would bite.

Huge bandages swathed what I'd yet to discover
(peeling them off in a hot bath, or bed)
that white stained to red, red to scarlet: a lover
lived there where no skin was, and his name was blood.

Who dirtied the water... No name for that thick hand
of panic that grabs you, that weird tête-à-tête
when the stuff that you're made of coils out of your limbs and
drops faster than poppies that flame in the wheat.

Six months convalescent. A gay chap in Worthing
came into my bedroom one hot summer's night.
He talked low, his hand talked some more with my farthing.
I fought him off briefly, then swooned out of sight.

Still, the sex that I dreamed of was not mine but other,
the one with the clothes and the rivery walk
such as Dawn, of 4A, whose pleats swung together,
whose melt-waters flooded our desert of talk.

By fifteen I'd choked on my schooldays, and legged it
off into a newsroom, and got my first pay.
My lord god was *copy*: to carry and fetch it
whenever the telex had something to say

or subs wanted feeding with stories and headlines.
Between whiles, I read like a man at the plough.
They shouted *Boy!* fruitlessly. I was with Anna,
with Jim on the bridge, or in Cannery Row.

And as I grew thinner and fainter and lighter
reading my way round the planets and back
my two fingers had an affair: the typewriter!
Discreet as a Madame in funeral black

my Underwood showed me the ropes, how you primed it
with bond and with carbons, with physical jerks,
how you buried your life in its armour, two-timed it
with letters, words, paragraphs, chapters... the works!

For ten years I rose and I fell in employment,
clerk, navvy, photographer, driver, male char.
I circled the globe now for real, with enjoyment,
young snapper of trifles, and bought my first car.

The bonnet stretched clear out of Hampshire to Dorset,
a model with Silverstone stamped on its heart.
Its owners would fill up, and rev it, and course it
then dump it for auction in any old mart.

It took up the space of an army division
and seated just two, boy and girl, as per ads.
The dash was of walnut, the lines beyond reason
a reason for living at speed, like the gods...

Ash-blond, heavy-chested, long-lidded, complaisant,
I picked out a beauty who'd let you – but all
my long words and bravado became detumescent
when faced with the other weird face of a girl

unknowing you needed some help with your outfit,
oblivious to foreplay as business to bard,
who thought that you'd just go about and about it
like Athos or d'Artagnan waving his sword.

Well the miracle hung out a signboard – postponed.
One world war was over, a cold one begun.
I climbed from my soapbox. The last siren tromboned.
Brits out, said the slogans. Beneath the bright sun

came the Fifties, the Sixties, came Suez and gunfire;
personal and public twined up the Last Post.
The state withered further and further from Empire.
The blaze of my childhood was over at last.

Elegiacs

Our finest hour is on the box again.
The B. of B. Dunkirk. Our bald Demosthenes.
The fishing-smack armada. Broken men
trapped on a beach, and Europe on its knees.

It's the longest hour I almost can remember:
fifty years, backs to that mythic wall.
The hellish shambles, set in pretty amber,
still sells a million thrills to one and all.

Since then there's Northern Ireland, Cuba, Suez,
Malaya, Burma, Cyprus and Korea,
fierce Mau Mau terrorists, or freedom fighters.
More backs to walls, more squaddies numb with fear.

But Dunkirk's number one. Close on its heels
the Spitfires scramble. Silk-scarfed to a man
a thousand Rupert Brookes write vapour trails
signed 'sacrifice' and 'Gallant little England'.

No fool would spit on that. No fool would stalk
the cenotaph, where death is mummified,
wrapped up for keeps in toothless rhetoric,
the ghostly Everyman of national pride.

His stony feet bleed poppies. Every day
the fallen fall a little more, but not
that brightly mythic hour. That's here to stay.
Stuck like a medal in an old man's throat.

Fieldwork

There's a r-r-r-repetitive bit
in Clementi's Op.25 no.1
which always has me wondering
briefly whether the needle's
stuck, till I remember it's a CD.
I remember then how I bring
the vinyl past along with me

whether I want to or not.
I brought patience too, as when
my first record player
(it cost a bomb, and weighed a ton)
stubbornly failed to get an explosion
out of Beethoven's *Pastoral*
and I sat there in the cold

front room waiting for
the excitement that never came,
the big boom-boom
I thought it was music's job
to provide. Eventually I caught up
with that sonic breeze meandering
over the fields, the serio-comic
birds, the river of chords.

This is music's job, to hitch up
pleasant feelings and march them
towards dissolution. That's why
the record goes round and round,
the tape spools, the CD spins
like a star. Here's you ploughed
under, sorted, born again.

In the CD Shop

'Quantity is competitive. Quality is complementary.'
– Dietrich Bonhoeffer

Rack upon rack of music
  – the visceral art –
from Hildegard of Bingen
  to Arvo Pärt.

You would need several lifetimes,
  each one profane,
just to slit open
  the clear cellophane

and drink notes. Not even my lust
  stretches to that.
The complete me backs off
  'The Complete Bach',

Elgar's 'Pomp and Circumstance',
  Liszt's fretful boast.
Consumer I may be but
  no wide-eyed Faust

wanting it all. I just like to know
  it's there in the shop.
Angels defend me
  from buying the lot!

Vacance

He sits in his sun-lounger in Provence
up in the hills where the cork trees grow
dark as the patina on tuppence,
empty of all he used to know.

The arm-rests tilt him down and back
(ingenious, these leisure engineers)
and the sun curves slowly around the stomach
that's just as happy as it appears.

A field of yellow stretches away
beneath closed lids, horizonless,
Locke's *tabula rasa*, plain as day,
unprofitable as this sacrifice

of time and money and treasure trove
acquired over dozens of head-down years,
the great god bullying above
and the little skirling airs

playing like insects on his skin,
stirring the root of him, floating there
on the bed of himself, in the eye of the sun,
with swallows cutting the dry blue air.

For she's there, face down, lost in a glade
where the ant and the lizard toil and glide,
the novel flung down at her side,
each naked hip an unsheathed blade.

Fresh

Fresh from swimming and the shower,
in cable-stitch and clogs, you come
to make a present of your hair
and shameless ankles to this poem.

Our Gang

The men have arrived, raucous as parrots,
in combustible yellow and hard hats.

They draw up lorries in a stockade.
It's some to an engine, some to a spade,

some to set up traffic lights and cones.
One reaches, gunwise, for his mobile phone.

Three shout, two whistle, one looks at the sky.
The men have arrived, to build or destroy

no one's quite sure what. It looks as though
they mean to part the cars, like the Red Sea,

and walk across, erect. Some of them shout
still puzzling over that angelic note

sent down to Adam at his place of work:
swing a shovel and the earth will speak.

The beetles come out...

The beetles come out late at night
when I am reading
some transcendent work
of the imagination. They seem
to have a special liking
for the old patchwork rug
down by the fire,
They rush in and out of it importantly:
letters
that have sprung off the page
and elected for another life altogether,
one of such authentic toil and trouble
that it requires more pairs of legs
than a slave-galley has oars.

Oh don't mind us, they say.
You carry on as usual.

I panic them into a fake Etruscan
cup, usually, and toss them out
into the dark.

I am striking...

I am striking at the slope
over and over with my heavy mattock.
This has put an ache in my back
which will ebb away over dinner.
More importantly it has cleared a way
down to the trees, the saplings
that will have to go and the two big limes
with a sycamore in between.
You can't see the trunks for
the bushes of pubic twigs, the overhanging dress
of leaves. Nevertheless I shall build a seat
down there, a lime-tree bower, cobbled
together in the ghostly grey of dead wood.

Skywriting

Saw the meteors last night
streaking across a cold sky.
They came where I wasn't looking,
a match-flare, a sudden zip,
one skating fast over Scotland,
one a flare over my shoulder.
Like tiny lucifers they came,
like a scalpel, like hair-raising incisions
on space. Then a fox barked
in the next-door field –
or was it a deer? –
an owl
gonged out his doomy cry,
trying me out for fear,
the black nimbus, the voice
nailing every leaf with frost.

English Zen

A warm wind drifts down the Isel valley,
carting off seedheads, tugging my arm
with its luscious pastoral sympathy
and the cuckoo's comical 'Here I am'.
Plaintive too, a call that absorbs
distance into its heart like rain
so we've two valleys to walk towards,
a probable English Zen

where the eyelets of our walking boots
are furred with green for ever and ever
and minds are rattled under their slates
by the ram-stam of the river.
It drags at the meadow's root and footing.
A staff of life. Old snake in the grass.
The back-flick hums a perfect nothing
as the fisherman makes his cast.

Friends

Two of them have gone ice-climbing in Norway.
Two are in Peru, where buses toil up the face
of the sky and thieves sting like the sun.
Julian is painting rock as it rears
up on its hind legs in the Himalayas.
Chris and Sylvia are rushing
round the museums and jazz clubs in New York
improvising responses, wondering which jumbo sandwich
in the deli to make an attempt on.
Michael is in Vilnius with map and Milosz
in one hand, the Good Hotel Guide in the other,
feeling his way to what he really feels
about a history that is his not his,
a city smelted in *Judenhetze.*
Here it just rains. Books grow in piles
round my chair like stalagmites, or mildew
on the shelves, packed in together country by country,
        the steppe
hard by the magic mountain, geography
melting into the fist that held the pen.
They'll be back soon to tell me all about it.
Then we'll relapse into fond absence, shuffling
along in the ruts of our own shoes.
When I think of ice-picks I think of Trotsky.

The Emigrant

to Diana Hendry

You are exchanging all things soft, south-west, and drowsy
such as sniffing the topmost pear in the kitchen bowl,
the laid-back thump, as the nights grow light with reggae
and Darcy Bussell soars through Colston Hall,

or stirring your cappuccino over a coffin
– the bookcase ones, that double up for death –
with Paula, in retro beads and caftan,
or floating the mind out over disbelief

where Brunel arches a solid Victorian eyebrow
from cliff to airy cliff, and Leigh Woods spans
the cracks that open up in the student ego

for Edinburgh, the Athens of the North:
Avon's water meadows and dying swans
for the nip and tuck of the blasts of the Firth of Forth.

Envoi

I think I mean you're brave, Diana.
        Brave to bundle all your treasure up
and hoist it on a stick and red bandana!

Women do that, restless to a man.
        Women are your only tramps.
Men stick at home, and lick their postage stamps.

Yes But

Why did Samuel Johnson get so goddam snippy
about Milton's *Lycidas* – 'of which the diction
is harsh, the rhymes uncertain, and the numbers unpleasing…
Where there is room for fiction
there is little grief.' Worse yet, 'the most awful
and sacred truths' are turned loose, unlawful-
ly romping about with nymphs and swains
in rumpled beds of pastoral.
'There is no nature, for there is no truth.'
So much for a cataclysmic grief.
So much for the most complete tour
of a man's insides since the storm-pelted Lear.

Let's put Sam's phenomenal head down
on the couch, ignoring for the moment
its resemblance to a Palaeolithic blunt instrument.
Let's dive into him with our Viennese aqualung
and see what lies on the seabed of his choler.
I spy a page of his *Life of Richard Savage.*
In the pious abrasions of his knees
I find black nights of hopelessness and rage.
That Protestant loathing of metaphor seems
to have broken out in carbuncles,
in obtuse and yappy fundamentalist screams
about art's provenance in wicked or in dirty dreams.

What's more there's that Miltonic proem
on *the ruine of our corrupted Clergy then*
in their height – red rag to a bull
for the cloth is sacred, even on a fool.
The state's the state! And the church is the church!
Cut to Boswell for the foam on the lips,
the bulging eye, the incontrovertible sneer
at the nonconformist and the leveller,
both scoundrels, both crazed enough to shake down
crowns and mitres. And the self-made man!

Somehow you can't see the two great scribes
ever quite making it up. Sam has a huff
the size and smell of his greatcoat. John
is capering on alone up Parnassus,
        which he calls Truth,
blind to the pitted raptures on his face.
When I bang their heads together
they are still bawling out
across rooms, bookshelves, centuries. They
roar through the bindings about what is
sacred, something too in Latin phrases
about brick and marble,
and human nature gone to hell.

Burdens

The cat who walked by himself
    was Kipling through and through.
The singsong hymn and the wise child Kim
    were Rudyard Kipling too.

He sang of the far-flung empire,
    its fever and its chill.
The pagan creeds and the lesser breeds
    were grist to his Sussex mill.

If you want to know how an engine pumps
    or an elder talks to a stripling
or why a soldier gets down in the dumps
    attend to Mr Kipling.

There's a wise old glint in his eye;
    there's a childish chant of a phrase.
As you flip the page there's sexual rage
    and the God of works and days.

And the Buddha, who smiles and smiles,
    and the sahib dead in his boots
and the nameless voice in the jungle
    that howls and screams and hoots.

Take up the white man's burden,
    the smartest PR move
since the snake was put in the garden
    to take the rap for love.

The more you look at it, the more
    that phrase feints and surprises:
it cleans as it sweeps as it kneels as it weeps
    as it kills as it 'civilises'.

He's a thorn in the foot of the thinker.
  The sun hardly ever sets
on one of his phrases – the sort of a stinker
  we'd like to leave at the vet's.

Love and Resistance

I think of two old women in Moscow,
Anna, 'the girl of the clever hello'

withering into Nadezhda's stare, that
battered old sphinx with a cigarette.

Into the whirlwind, adjusting a hem.
No end of riddles love threw at them

and they stuck to its bristly hide like burrs,
the party of rememberers…

Anna: the poet Anna Akhmatova.
Nadezhda: Mandelstam's widow.
Into the Whirlwind: title of a Gulag memoir by Evgenia Ginzburg.

Cut Short

after Corbière: *Idylle coupée*

They come from the cops, or a cheap hotel –
either one will lend them a cell.
Their songs are ripe, and out of tune,
pitched in the key of a waning moon.

I sit and watch them, radiating
couldn't-care-less in neck and wrist.
They turn on their heel with a sudden swing
which gives my guts a bit of a twist.

Young as twelve – or thirty – or fifty –
ex-post-facto virgins, unless
balding, painted, iffy and whiffy,
a trifle handled about the chest.

Young men buy them drinks in bars,
although distinctly nervous,
apprentices to those amours
snuffed out in the marriage service.

The girls solicit who they can:
the squaddy, farmer, businessman –
but not the boyos in the arts
with empty pockets and bleeding hearts!

God's sent these girls to keep maids pure
and free from sexual hunters;
they form a *cordon sanitaire*
around the pimps and punters

from dusk to dawn. And that's not all
their useful application.
Backed up like frescos to the wall
or the crosses of the station

they soak up all our sins, they kiss
the night air in the underpass,
they come off shift dead-beat pietàs
only to smile like Violettas.

Suddenly old Death starts up –
mine not to wonder why –
crepuscular, from his ingle nook
in the back of the seeing eye

and points a crooked finger
at her soul, her wasted youth,
where my looks only linger
on the mole beside her mouth.

Beatitudes I never tried.
Sweats that only sweated and dried.

There's a law, however, in every case,
and a God for guys like us:
with half an eye to a pert young Miss
I was run over by a bus.

Protest

For I have noticed that British poets leave the Troubles to
the Irish.
For they are better at it than we are.
For nothing goes down so well in the home counties as wit.
For they are fond of a leg-pull in the north also.
For a poet mustn't be seduced by journalism.
For Jane Austen never looked up to see the Napoleonic wars.
For we must not be violated by an idea, nor descend to
taking a stand.
For we are instructed that history is at an end.
For the firebombers and refugees only take up seconds,
between the Dow Jones and the weather.
For we don't speak the language, either of Kosovo or of
Armagh.
For breasts are glowing on the top shelves, whereas the
charity shop is up a side alley.
For the purpose of irony is to strip the cogs.
For all *siècles* must have a *fin*.
For the fireworks music will be by Andrew Lloyd Webber.
For the poets have decommissioned themselves, in advance
of the talks.

Not Dark Yet

So here it is at last, the distinguished thing,
  in Faber's tasteful livery:
Simon Armitage's mini millennium poem,
  a thousand years of history
got up in *fin de siècle* modes of thought,
  chiefly headline stories and jokes
about wisdom not stopping to take off its coat,
  about money and fakes,
the world and its web according to Bill Gates,
  business pocketing its percents
on everything from soya beans and kalashnikovs
  to silicon breast implants,
how news isn't news without live-to-camera
  wide-eyed sincerity tropes,
how tragedy falls as snow but turns to slush
  in mini-series and docu-soaps.
So what can we read between these crafty lines,
  how interpret the state of the nation
from a fast run-through of these sparkling runes and rhymes
  that don't, or hardly. Fashion,
TV news, raw footage of yet another war,
  a famine, a river of refugees,
smart missiles, smoking rubble, smart metaphors
  for collateral damagees.
Balloonists, millennium babies (the conceiving of),
  football, trains, astronomers,
those heavenly bodies poets traditionally love,
  American high-school killers.
It's all exciting. And it's all a bloody mess.
  But at least you don't subscribe
to 'the complicated shame of Englishness'
  diagnosed by a number of our tribe
who think we should own up and take the rap
  for all our fathers' sins
such as painting the world red when it was black,
  brown, yellow, etc; colonialism

at home and abroad, greed disguised as a mission
  to civilise nations;
greed, power, the age-old missionary position;
  sheer exploitation.
They look with envy across the north Atlantic
  and the Irish sea,
wishing their own loyalties were less fragmented,
  wanting an 'identity'
that doesn't involve idiocies of class and rank
  or waving a disputed flag,
one that apparently they haven't yet found
  and others apparently have.
I have some sympathy with this. But not too much.
  Do I detect a cultural cringe
in that complicated, almost theological anguish
  for the vinegar and sponge
of expiation?... As though we must be crucified for ever
  by what some did and said;
as though this hara-kiri on St George's spear
  was yet another crusade.
Well I'm not racing up to that high moral ground,
  the white man's burden.
I'd sooner sit cross-legged with Nusrat Khan
  praising God. Or dig my garden.
I'm glad to belong to the race of Orwell and Donne,
  Fielding, William Blake.
If we don't yet have righteousness in Albion
  at least it's not a burning lake.
We've been home to Conrad, Eliot, Henry James,
  Yeats, Rushdie, Marx and Freud.
They liked it here, for all its royal philistines
  and barbarous food.
I like it too, its clouds, its thousand and one
  diffusions of light,
its clubs and pubs, its technicoloured young
  strobing every summer night
in tight white miniskirts and handkerchief tops
  brief as a dare,

the boys in jeans and tee-shirts, with a ton
of hair-gel on their spiky hair.
What else? I like the Early Music Movement,
Damien Hirst, Patrick Marber's nous.
I like the cosmological hullabaloo of looking
out into early space.
I like the million and one societies dedicated to
the pursuit of this and that
from the Friends of the Hunting of the Snark
to the welfare of the common bat.
I like *Gregory's Girl, Brassed Off, Trainspotting*.
I like the way
we open up, eventually, to other cultures
even as we snort out our dismay.
I like the nonconformist turn of mind, the wit
that keeps our rulers semi-sane,
the changing patterns in the national carpet.
I even like the Dome
those whingers hate, as though it isn't cricket
to have a knees-up when the end is nigh,
it's downright wicked.
Bad luck to the writhers. When we cease to praise
we'll surely die.
I see black wings. I see our 'complications' as
a case of terminal irony,
jeering become a flag, the doubters hung
up on their own inverted pride,
a squall of Uriah Heeps, taken to standing
too long on their head.

Does this make me a reactionary old fart,
wailing like Bob Dylan:
'She's gone with the man in the long black coat',
gone to rack and ruin –
'she' being the civilisation once held dear,
that rule of law
which threw up Newton, Purcell, Shakespeare,
Turner, Dickens, Wren and Moore?

Don't get me started! I'm not one to shout
  about this sceptred isle
except when semi-demi Gilberts and bonehead Georges
  move in for the kill.
One more post-skill installation and I'm off
  to sounding shores.
Give the twentieth century my crooked love.
  This next one's yours.

Lonely Hearts

Queuing up in the flesh
at the latter end
of *The New York Review of Books*
they try on the glass slipper of words.

The animal that likes narration
is up on its hind legs
begging to be let out. Or in.
(Oh the enchanted hollow trees
of Manhattan!)

Here is the real them,
sympatico, well-heeled, sincere.
Warm and sexy, but especially warm,
with Oppenheimer's cranium
and Woody Allen's charm.

There but for the long winter
of an English heart
go you and I, spanking over the foam
oh surely to fetch
the king's daughter home.

You've heard it...

You've heard it a thousand times in the movies.
It covers a lot of emotional ground.
When the train in the night starts a-blowin'
and nobody knows where it's comin' or goin'...
they really do make that lonesome sound.

Lonesome and punctilious. Who'll make whole
the driver, and his box-car soul?

The Bed Artist

No not John and Yoko
twittering away in their bird's nest hair
like an Edward Lear drawing come to life;
not Heine on his mattress-grave either,
pierced and printed by his own skeleton;
not Oblomov curled up forever
in his Russian nightcap
against the cold light of Asia Minor;
nor the transcendent pillow-fight
in Jean Vigo's *Zéro de Conduite;*
not Rip van Winkle or the Sleeping Beauty
crackling in their cellophane;
nor Coleridge's pleasure-dome
with the invisible price-tags
such as nightmares and constipation
and those unspeakable brass clyster-pipes
evacuating him to Malta;
not the rank enseamèd sheets,
not the dormouse, but the view
day after day from the bower of pain,
the sickness unto death,
little wreaths and posies stabbing out
from the back, the neck, the groin,
the cerebellum.

You have to arrange yourself
around your own sentence
as best you can.

Milk for the Pussens

We have been adopted by a black cat
with a white bib and paws.
Almost a designer cat,
who pushes his affections
into your stomach as though
he was making bread.
He's come from nowhere,
the exact spot you yourself are headed for.

Black Movie

The bone scan machine moves
at the speed of Omar's moving finger.
What it writes you don't want to know.
Hot spots all over your rather pretty
miniaturised skeleton, which shows up
sepia, and then, alas, talks dirty in black.